The Honeysuckle Blue and Other Parables

by
Stephen E. Smith

with illustrations
by
Glen Rounds

St. Andrews Press
Laurinburg, North Carolina

Library of Congress Cataloging-in-Publication Data

Smith, Stephen E., 1946-. The honeysuckle shower and other parables / Stephen E. Smith. Illustrations by Glen Rounds--Laurinburg, N.C. St. Andrews Press, 1987.

I. Rounds, Glen. II. Title

ISBN 0-932662-72-2   87-061593

Acknowledgments

Sections of this book were first published by *Pembroke Magazine*, *Abraxas*, *The Wilmington Review*, This End Up Broadsides, and Friends of the Library, North Carolina Wesleyan College.

The author wishes to thank the North Carolina Arts Council and the National Endowment for the Arts for a grant which made the writing of this book possible.

Special thanks to Betty Reep and Rick Lewis.

to Raymond Tyner

Contents

I The Honeysuckle Shower

II Pipes and Such

III Sheer Lace Curtains

The Honeysuckle Shower
and
Other Parables

I

The Honeysuckle Shower

The Honeysuckle Shower

The boy lived in a room in an old boarding house. The house was sided with cedar shakes and roofed with red tin that panged soothingly during the long rainy winter nights and the bathroom had a wavy green glass window that stretched the length of the shower and so in late March when the wind lifted lightly the sheer lace curtains which the landlord's beautiful, big-breasted wife hung out to dry, he opened the shower window and began thus to share his bath with vines, green tendrils creeping closer, strangling the shower head, tangling between the sashes, drifting imperceptively up the tile walls, until one April afternoon the vines bloomed honeysuckle and the sky rose deep blue beyond the window and when the boy stepped nude into that meadow the steam drifted into the finely-veined leaves and the blossoms, thick and sweet as cream, rattled all about him.

The boy was just eighteen and had been reading a romantic mountain poet for whom it was always spring, and so he began to dance a mountain dance, twisting, turning, stomping, singing and dancing as he never had before, not a soul to see him, not a soul to care. There was, as always and of course, a war somewhere and he began to wonder why anyone would go to the trouble, why anyone would desire a moment beyond this: the pure exultation of singing and dancing in the shower. Soon, however, broken blossoms clogged the drain and water flooded the floor and the landlord began banging on the door and a bee, dazed by the perfume and angered by the water, which by now had turned cold, stung the boy on the temple, tumbling him backward out of the shower.

Just then the landlord, a garrulous war veteran and inveterate beer drinker who smelled faintly of bay rum and urine, kicked open the door. He had seen many springs come and go, and he knew just what to do: he turned off the water, ripped down the honeysuckle, slammed shut the window and swatted the bee. "I do not understand this!" the landlord blurted. The naked boy tried to explain what he had been feeling about spring and honeysuckle and war and lace curtains lifting lightly and cedar shakes and the sound of rain on a red tin roof and romantic mountain poems, but the landlord did not want to listen. Moreover, he had not read any romantic mountain poems and did not care to. He, in fact, disliked poetry. He simply said, "Listen up you little fuzzball: there are moments, now and then, when this life is entirely too cloying."

The Hard Lesson

When the landlord was a small boy he learned a lesson. It was a hard lesson, but it stood him in good stead all his life. Here is what happened.

The landlord was coming home from school one day when three bigger boys stopped him on a street corner and demanded a nickel. "You must pay us a nickel or we will stick you with this needle," said the biggest boy, holding up the needle to glint in the sunlight. The landlord did not have a nickel and he did not want to get stuck by the needle, so he ran like hell. The four bigger boys pursued him to the front porch where his father waited.

The landlord's father, who was known for his quick temper, spanked him severely. "You must not run away from a fight," his father said. "I do not care if they beat you bloody; you must not run away. Do you understand?"

"Yes," the landlord replied.

The next afternoon the three bigger boys waited on the corner. They were laughing. All day the landlord had concealed a piece of 10-inch galvanized pipe in his shirt. When the boys demanded two nickels, he laid the pipe up side their heads. He broke one boy's nose; he knocked out the teeth of another; the third got a bloody lip. Then they all ran away. Satisfied, the landlord dropped the pipe and strolled home.

His father was waiting on the front porch. His father's face was crimson. "Three bloody boys told me that you beat them with a pipe. Is this true?" his father asked.

"Yes," he said proudly, "I did."

His father spanked him severely. "You must never do that again," his father said. "Do you understand me?"

"Yes," the landlord replied.

But really the landlord did not understand. He did not understand then, and he did not understand now. Not understanding was a hard lesson, but it had stood him in good stead all his life.

Balls

The boy was confused. He would awaken at night and stare out the window at the sheer lace curtains hanging on the clothesline--silent gauzy ghosts the landlord's beautiful, big-breasted wife had emasculated--and he'd wonder at the source of his uneasiness. He'd switch on his bedroom light and read lines written by a romantic mountain poet. It was always spring in those poems and it seemed logical that the answer should one day make itself known.

It did. But it was not lines written by any poet that assuaged the boy's misery; rather, it was his landlord, a talkative man who drank too much beer and often gave advice without invitation.

On this particular day the landlord was quite angry with the boy. The bathroom was flooded, vines were growing up the walls, insects had begun to swarm, and the boy, having been stung by a bee, was lying naked on the floor. The landlord helped the boy to his feet. "What the hell has taken holt of you?" he asked.

"I don't know," the boy said, swaying unsteadily, then collapsing, his slick buttocks producing a rude squeal on the edge of the porcelain tub and a chill knifing deep into his groin. The boy struggled to regain his composure and attempted to explain, talking in short, stutterish bursts of emotion. He went on about how much he liked living in the landlord's house--the red tin roof, the cedar shakes, the sheer lace curtains hung in the cool breeze to dry. It was the spring of his eighteenth year and he talked of the war and how futile it all seemed. But because he did not know what he was saying--did not, in fact, know who or where he was--he made absolutely no sense. The landlord shook his head and said, "You make absolutely no sense."

"That's exactly what's wrong," the boy said. "Nothing makes any sense." The landlord could not disagree. He had arrived at the same conclusion many years before when he'd awakened to find the beautiful, big-breasted nurse who was now his wife stroking his brow. Often he'd recall those days before the war when he was a handsome boy standing naked in a line with other boys who were so anxious for life.

Just then the lingering perfume of honeysuckle crept into the landlord's nostrils and he happened to look out through the vine-covered window into a sky that rose deep blue. "I know what it is," the landlord cried, pointing at the boy's crotch. "You've got balls!"

The Blessing in Disguise

The landlord was a talkative man with a quick temper, a bad back and no balls. Loquaciousness he had inherited from his mother, a kind but truly stupid woman who discoursed constantly on subjects about which she knew nothing. The quick temper and bad back were gifts from his father, a normally tolerant man who was forced by an intemperate wife and a ruptured disk into moments of unbridled rage. The landlord's balls had quite simply been blown off in the war.

The landlord did not remember much about what had happened to his balls. One day he was a handsome young man standing naked in a line with a doctor's fingers tickling his nuts and the next day he was waking up in a hospital bed minus the above mentioned genitalia and feeling dangerously surprised. A beautiful, big-breasted nurse was standing over him, stroking his forehead and repeating gently, "You're all right now; you're just fine."

Which, of course, he was not. And when he discovered that his balls had gone God knows where, he screamed and the beautiful, big-breasted nurse buried his face deep in her remarkable cleavage and whispered, "You'll never miss them; they weren't good for much anyway."

Which--fortunately or unfortunately?--turned out to be true. He married the nurse, who liked to cradle his talkative face in her bosom but who, because of her rich Catholic upbringing, cringed when she thought that the hard part of any man might someday penetrate her pinkage. On the first night of their honeymoon she sighed and squealed as he sucked. "You know," she said afterwards, "the war was truly a blessing in disguise."

It was then she discovered the landlord's quick temper.

The Right Medicine

The landlord always used bay rum on his hair. After he toweled his hair dry, he'd shake a little bay rum into his palm, rub his hands together briskly, and run his fingers through his hair. Bay rum had a sweet smell which the landlord liked.

The landlord's wife hated bay rum. It had a sweet smell that turned her stomach. For years she pleaded with her husband not to use bay rum, but it seemed the more she pleaded the more bay rum he used.

One day she asked the landlord why he persisted in using the bay rum when she had requested that he not.

"Just to piss you off," he replied, smiling.

The landlord's wife got an idea. When the landlord had gone, she put a funnel in the bottle of bay rum and urinated just enough to deaden the sweet smell.

That'll fix him, she thought.

The next morning the landlord toweled his hair dry, splashed some bay rum into his palm, rubbed his hands together briskly and ran his fingers through his hair. He took a deep breath and smiled.

"Ah," he said, "there's nothing sweeter than a familiar scent."

The Highway to Anywhere

The boy had never been with a woman. He was painfully shy and women made him feel awkward and ashamed, so he had never, beyond an errant kiss or two stolen from a blushing girl who had once spun a cola bottle in his direction, had much to do with them. After all, he was but eighteen years of age and there was plenty of time to partake of the pleasures of life. Or at least that's what everyone told him.

"That's your trouble," the landlord said, helping the naked boy to his feet. And he went on to explain how a woman might solve his problem--how a woman, given the correct circumstances and the proper timing, could put his mind at ease and allow him to sleep soundly through these early spring nights when the peepers and bullhumpers called from the poplars and creeks. "What you need," the landlord said, "is a piece of ass."

The next morning the boy phoned a girl he knew and asked her to a drive-in movie. The landlord smiled and punched the boy in the shoulder. "You can use my car," he said.

The landlord's car was nothing to look at. The tires were badly worn, the windshield was cracked, the seats were sprung and the gas gauge had not moved in ten years (for emergencies, the landlord had to keep a smelly five gallon can of gasoline in the back seat). But the landlord and the boy spent the day waxing the car and polishing the chrome. They vacuumed the carpets and washed the windows, and if the car did not compare to the flashy models driven by other boys, well, it was good enough. The boy was cheerful and eager.

"You're all set?" the landlord asked.

"All set," the boy answered.

"You'll need this to protect your plumbing," the landlord said, slipping him a condom. "Remember to leave some room in the tip and make especially sure this gasket don't leak."

The boy nodded and put the condom into his pocket.

The landlord patted the boy's shoulder. "Look out there," he said. "Look at that sky."

The boy looked. The sun was beginning to set and the horizon was tinted a deep pink. The cool air was vivid with nightsounds. The boy started the engine. It purred.

The landlord smiled. "Just remember," he said, "this is your night; the highway to anywhere is wide open."

New Shoes

for Rick Lewis

It was dusk. As the boy guided the landlord's car carefully round the corner, the headlights flickered among the dogwood blossoms and caught a child running. The child--he could not tell if it was a boy or a girl--hung suspended in the high beams for only a moment--no more than two or three strides--before the car's forward motion carried the lights down the dark macadam. But that moment was time enough for the boy to recognize that the running child had on new tennis shoes. The white rubber soles winked in the rear-view mirror.

The boy smiled. He remembered how each spring his mother had taken him to buy a new pair of tennis shoes, how in the corner shop that smelled faintly of leather and canvas they'd plundered among the boxes and untangled tissue until a pair of new tennis shoes slipped neatly onto the boy's small feet. When the boy stood up in those new shoes, he knew it was spring! The dark, sodden weight of winter all gone--almost as if the earth had fallen away in celebration, the air drifting him softly skyward.

The boy wondered if the child he'd seen running was late for supper, wondered if the child was even now brushing through hedges, leaping over fences, cutting down some dark alley to find a kitchen light left burning by a mother who understood that a child has no knowledge of time on a spring night when he's been running in new tennis shoes. The boy could see the child easing open the screen door, could see him stepping ever so lightly, the soft white soles silent on the blue linoleum.

The boy stopped the car in front of the girl's house. The house was dark. He sat for a moment, resting his forehead on the steering wheel, and wondered why it was his feet had grown so heavy.

The Girl with Golden-Red Hair

The landlord wondered what was happening to the boy.
From the moment the boy backed the car carefully out of the driveway-- the gears grinding slightly as he eased it into low--the landlord had wondered. He watched the brake lights wink red as the car rounded the corner, and he wondered how long it would take the boy to drive to the girl's house. The landlord went into the kitchen and put some ice and a cold six-pack of beer into a cooler. Then he wandered into the back yard where his wife had hung out her sheer lace curtains to dry. He sat down under a blossoming dogwood.

The more beer he drank, the more he wondered. He wondered if the boy had picked up the girl, wondered if she weren't even now sliding into the car--his car--her blouse slightly asunder and her long silky legs ruffling the corduroy seat covers. With one hand she tucked her skirt neatly beneath her buttocks and with the other she lifted a slender beringed finger to her forehead, scolding a stray curl into place. God! she had such red hair--golden-red. And her eyes: they were so blue, a translucent blue, a blue languid as the late evening sky.

The landlord drank four more beers and waited patiently. It was dark and growing very cool, but the boy would need time. Let him fumble, let him find his way. He looked at his watch. No doubt they were at the drive-in, no doubt the boy had eased the girl down onto the seat. No doubt his hand was inching up her thigh. She might resist--yes, she was resisting--but just enough to maintain her respectability. She did not want to discourage him. And now his fingertips were entwined in curls of golden-red hair!

There, you're home, the landlord thought, plunging his hand deep into the cooler for that last can of ice-cold beer.

The Good Question

The drive-in movie was about teenagers at the beach who danced in the sand to rock bands whose electric instruments were not plugged in and there was a motorcycle gang comprised of surly, disadvantaged youths who just wanted to be friendly.

The girl was indeed very friendly. She had seen this particular beach movie the previous night, and twenty minutes into the feature, the boy had managed to remove her scanties and was fumbling with the condom given him by the landlord.

It was, of course and as always, over very quickly. The boy dropped the used condom into the back seat, and he and the girl sat busily adjusting snaps and belts and buttons, twisting their bodies this way and that.

During the intermission the girl excused herself to the restroom, and the boy began to worry about the condom. Had it leaked? He had, of course, heard stories of defective rubbers, of lives altered irrevocably. Would he now spend his nights tossing and turning, nagged by the possibility of premature parenthood? He climbed into the back seat, tipped over the five gallon gasoline can kept there for emergencies, filled the condom till it was the size of a basketball and held it up, its faintly luminous contents silhouetted against the giant screen.

Good God! here was a universe whose existence he had never suspected. Millions of polliwog sperm suspended in a mythical ether, a cosmos of petroleum. He could imagine each phlegm-like strand of semen a galaxy populated by a billion worlds--life and death, good and evil, etc.--the sorrowful struggle of so many sad souls--the moons and stars, the milky ways and supernovas! He touched the undulating condom with his index finger and marveled at the waves of expanding disturbance. Tilting his head slightly sidewise, he considered the possibility that the world in which he existed hung by just such a tenuous thread. And if so, what then did any of it matter? Could he not, with the mere release of thumb and forefinger, with the tiniest electrical charge--nothing more than the most casual of random thoughts pulsed to a minuscule hank of muscle--send this universe crashing headlong into oblivion?

Just then the boy noticed a smear of muted color vibrating through the translucent fluid. And focusing his attention beyond the prophylactic, beyond the cracked windshield, beyond the autos angled randomly into the starry night sky, beyond the neon refreshment stand, beyond all whimsey, he could discern clearly a red, white and blue clown balancing a green ball with the number 1 suspended in a halo of pure white. An omnipresent voice was roaring in the darkness: "One more minute to visit our refreshment stand!"

What could it all mean? The boy, who had a somewhat metaphoric nature, was transfixed by the possible implications of what he beheld. Of course, the girl chose just this moment to return. She opened the car door and stared at the boy, who seemed oblivious to her presence. She was a worldly and practical girl who had observed, at this very drive-in theater, the headliners of more than a few rocking autos, and she had meticulously catalogued male reactions that ranged from profound grief to breathless exhilaration. She had, however, never happened upon a boy who watched junk food enticements through a spent condom brimming with gasoline. "Just what in God's name do you think you are doing?" she asked, not impolitely.

Old Shoes

Something was wrong. The boy sat on the edge of his unmade bed and could feel down deep in the darkish marrow of his bones that something was very wrong. Outside his open window a small wind foolishly bothered the dogwood blossoms, brushing them lightly against the patched, fly-specked screen. The boy knew that if ever there was a night he should sleep soundly, this was it. After all, what was there to worry him? What subtle injustice could possibly fret him on such an evening? It was, after all, a rare and beautiful night: the temperature was a silky 62 degrees, the sky was clear, his health was perfect--he, in fact, was somewhat subdued by the thought that he might never be more physically robust than he was at this moment--he was eighteen years old (could there be a better age?), and he had just nailed his first piece of ass. What in the world could possibly be wrong?

There was, of course, no kidding himself. The boy knew the source of his brooding: he had, in all likelihood, irreparably altered the course of someone's life. A casual turn in his own life, as traumatic as the prospect seemed, was a responsibility he could bear, but the idea of altering the direction of another's life was more than worrisome. He was thinking of the girl, thinking of her as an innocent he had led down the road to perdition. She was despoiled, ruined! And was he not the responsible party?

It was easy--perhaps best--to conceive of her only as a "piece of ass." Wasn't that what the landlord had called her? Was that not the expression used by the gum-smacking, shoulder-punching boys who gathered at the pool hall to boast in intimate detail of their latest conquests? A piece of ass. . . . In that way he need not

21

consider her flesh and blood, need not be burdened with a tiresome belief that she had any feelings about what had transpired between them, need not be bothered by the moral consequences of his stiff penetration into her soft body.

He was reminded of a girl he knew in high school, a coquettish yet innocent girl whose life had unravelled before his very eyes. She was not pretty--pretty girls never spent themselves for want of affection--and she came from a poor farm family who sent her to school on the first day of September in a starched print dress and new black and white saddle oxfords. "Hot snatch," "pecker bait," the other boys called her.

The other boys were, of course, correct. And all that year, as her reputation declined, the boy watched her. Her print dress faded to a doleful wash-water gray, hickeys the size and color of shit roaches blossomed on her neck, her hair grew long and disheveled, her blue eyes lost their luster. But more than anything he noticed her shoes, the black and white saddle oxfords that had, on that first day of September, shone with the simple good sense expected of the improvised.

In mid-October there appeared a random scuff or two, by November the laces had begun to fray, a December snow storm eradicated any absolute distinctions, and by January the bruised heels slumped in total dejection. It was common knowledge that any interested boy at the school could do with this poor girl as he pleased, could take her with, as everyone observed, the simple wink of an eye. Thus the boy imagined each Monday morning how, in the back seat of some car on the previous Saturday night, her faded print dress cast aside, she had, with the toe of one shoe, eased off the heel of the other, the oxford clunking to the floorboard with a sound as hollow as he felt. With February, a hole crept into one sole, and by April a small, wiggly pink toe--eager as a metamorphosed insect--escaped into the sunlight.

There were cold moments when the boy felt more pity for the shoes than he felt for the girl. Had they not been crafted by human hands with only the noblest of intentions? Were they not meant to keep their owner warm and safe? Why then had she, of all people, chosen to abuse such a gift?

One June afternoon when the boy was overcome by frustration and/or curiosity, he asked her these questions. And she looked at him in complete puzzlement. "What have my shoes got to do with anything?" she asked.

The boy was much taken aback. "Shoes tell all there is to know about a person," he said. "So goes the person, so go her shoes."

"Listen," she said, "I'm the best damn piece of ass around. If you're interested in a tumble, fine; if not, bug off!"

A small wind foolishly bothered the dogwood blossoms, brushing them lightly against the patched, fly-specked screen. The boy tried to recall the shoes worn by the girl to whom he'd made love this night, but oddly enough he could not. So he unlaced his brown oxfords and placed them carefully under the bed. He put his head down on the pillow and fell fast asleep.

II

Pipes and Such

Pipes and Such

The landlord loved his plumbing. He loved reducing wye branches and ground-joint unions. He loved compression nuts, swing check valves, slip couplings, drum taps, 1/4 double bends and taper seals. He loved the notion that hidden behind the walls and in the ceilings and under his feet, the substance of life was flowing silently to and fro, bringing refreshment and comfort, carrying away filth and evil. He loved the melodious gurgle of sweet, clear water.

The landlord had come to love plumbing in this way. After he was mustered out of the service, he used the money given him by a benevolent and grateful government in compensation for his self-sacrifice and suffering--and most notably for the loss of his male baggage--to buy a boarding house. It was a lovely boarding house roofed with red tin and sided with cedar shakes. It rested firmly on substantial brick piers in a lot shaded by poplar and elm interspersed with flowering dogwood. He had taken his new wife, a beautiful, big-breasted nurse he'd met during his lengthy convalescence, to live there. She also loved the house, loved the large grassy yard where, in the spring, she could hang out her sheer lace curtains to dry stiff in the fresh air. The landlord and his wife were very happy.

Until the day the pipes began to groan and hammer. The flushing of a toilet or the closing of a tap set the house to shaking and complaining with such intensity that it severely rattled the landlord's already fragile nerves. It seemed that his whole world--a world purchased with the sacrifice of his most vital possessions--was shaken (as in fact it was) to its very foundations. Thus it was that he set about to become a master plumber.

For three years, the landlord replaced plumbing. He learned the secrets of temperature and pressure; the subtleties of drainage, traps and venting; he learned pipe data--brass, copper, galvanized and cast-iron; he learned the use of wrenches and threaders, solder and flux; he learned how to drain, install, repair, and mount--but more than anything he learned to love the business of plumbing. He learned to love the warmth of molten lead and the texture of oakum caulked into an open joint. He learned to love the hiss of a cool ladle plunged into a plumber's furnace. He learned to love the angling of an asbestos joint needed to keep hot lead in a horizontal hub and the force with which to tamp the lead airtight. His nights and days were plumbing; his thoughts and dreams were plumbing. Those private moments when he ducked his head beneath the stiff, air-dried sheets to assuage his wife's desires, he was thinking always: pipes and hot metal.

Finally the day arrived when it was all complete. Everything was new--new drains, new toilets, new sinks, new faucets. He turned on the kitchen spigot and listened to the mellifluous gush of clear, fresh water. He beamed. "You cannot imagine what this moment means to me," he said. Then he turned off the tap.

The pipes hammered and groaned.

The wife smiled and eased her hand into his pants. "Well," she said, "nothing is ever perfect."

A Good Theory

After the pain in his back became too much to bear, the landlord went to a doctor who explained that there was something wrong with one of the landlord's legs and that he was standing crooked. "It's gravity," the doctor said. "You are suffering back pain because you are out of balance." The doctor sold the landlord a set of lifts for his shoes. One lift was thicker than the other. "These will put you in balance and the pain will go away."

The landlord wore the lifts in his shoes but the pain did not go away. In fact, it got worse. And to add to his discomfort, the landlord suffered from diarrhea. When he took the lifts out of his shoes, the diarrhea went away. When he put the lifts back in, the diarrhea returned.

So what was wrong with his back? The landlord decided that he'd figure it out for himself. After all, the body was no more than a house for the soul. It had plumbing and wiring, and the landlord knew that plumbing and wiring could be understood from books. So he went to the library and studied a book on the nervous system.

He learned that the thoracolumbar system begins in the lumbar portion of the spinal cord and that nerve impulses from the eyes pass along the sensory nerves to the brain and that the brain sends impulses down the motor nerves to the muscles in the back. The book stated that the eyes are full of sensory nerves and sensory nerves are subject to stimuli.

Could something be irritating the sensory nerves in his eyes? The landlord looked in the mirror and there was the answer: dandruff! Tiny flakes had fallen from his head into his eyebrows. Some of these flakes were, no doubt, drifting imperceptibly into his eyes and irritating nerve endings which in turn caused his back muscles to seize up.

The landlord rubbed bay rum into his scalp and within a week the dandruff was gone--and along with it his bad back! Bay Rum was the right medicine, and as long as the landlord used it daily, he did not suffer from back pain.

He kept a fresh bottle of bay rum in his medicine cabinet, right next to a rusty old funnel which was always sitting there for some reason.

Twice-Frozen Ice

The landlord's wife had this theory. She believed that ice should be frozen only once. If the ice in her ice cube tray melted, she did not put the tray with the old water back in the freezer to freeze again. That would have made twice-frozen ice, and twice-frozen ice was a very dangerous substance.

After she married the landlord, he discovered that she believed that twice-frozen ice was dangerous. "How could this be?" he questioned. "Water's water; everyone knows that. And ice is just frozen water. The only difference is the temperature. How could it be dangerous?"

"It just is," she said.

"How do you know?" he continued questioning.

"I just know, that's all."

The landlord was puzzled. "Listen," he said, "I'm the best plumber in this town and I can tell you that water is water. It freezes, it thaws and it freezes again and then it thaws. It's that simple."

"It's not that simple. Ice that has frozen twice will make you very ill. It might even be fatal. You should never ever use twice-frozen ice. Everybody knows that."

"Who is everybody?" the landlord asked. "I've never heard anyone speak of twice-frozen ice."

"Just everybody," she answered. "Everybody knows that you should never use twice-frozen ice."

The discussion continued for some time before the wife grew weary of trying to explain what she knew was true. "Okay, okay," she said finally, "you win. Twice-frozen ice is just ice, and ice is ice and water is water." And she took out all of her ice cube trays to thaw. "There," she said, "when the ice has melted we'll put the trays back to freeze. Are you satisfied?"

"Fine," the landlord said, and they both left the kitchen.

But when the ice had thawed, the wife sneaked back into the kitchen and emptied the trays. Very carefully she opened the tap. The tap had a tendency to groan and she was very careful not to make a sound. When the trays were full of fresh water, she put them back on the counter.

Just as soon as the wife left the kitchen, the landlord sneaked in and emptied the trays. He filled the trays with water from melted ice he had hidden in the cupboard and put the trays in the freezer.

That night the landlord and his wife had ice in their camomile tea. When their glasses were empty, the landlord asked, "How do you feel?"

"Just fine," she said. "You were right: ice is ice and water is water. There's not one bit of difference."

"Except the temperature," he reminded her with a smile.

The landlord's wife nodded and smiled back, gently.

The Day with No Song

When the boy awakened it was raining. The dogwood blossoms sagged against the patched, fly-specked screen in a most unspring-like fashion. It was a dull rain and did not pang soothingly on the red tin roof. The clothesline was bare.

The boy rolled over--the sheets were clammy, the pillow damp--and tried to read lines written by a romantic mountain poet for whom it was always spring. He read his most favorite poem, the poem that seemed to have been written just for him. But something was wrong. The romantic lines of the mountain poet had lost their lyric quality; his words wilted like blossoms in gray rain.

The boy scuffled around. He ate a cracker. He took a shower. He listened to inane love songs on a squawky radio. He changed clothes twice. He polished his shoes and discovered a hole in one sole and a glob of soggy, gray-blue gum stuck to the other.

He took in an afternoon movie about a garrulous war veteran and inveterate beer drinker who'd had his balls blown off and could not find happiness. There were bull fights and a lot of drinking, and it was impossible for the boy to give a damn about the characters. He had not known any like them, and he hoped he never would.

He wasn't hungry, so he wandered back to the boarding house and found that its cedar shakes were drizzle-stained a most unpleasant shade of brown. He opened the front door with much obvious commotion, knocking over an umbrella stand and stomping his feet, hoping to attract the landlord's attention. He wanted someone to talk to. "Don't you know how to enter a house properly?" the landlord screamed down the steps.

He plundered about his room, scoured out the rust-stained sink and discovered that the drain was sluggish. When he shut off the spigot the pipes groaned and hammered. He went to bed and read more lines by a romantic mountain poet for whom it was always spring. "Hell," he said to himself, "I can write as well as this." So he sat for an hour looking at a blank sheet of paper. Then he wrote a title: "Some Days Have No Song." He tried to write the poem, but the words just wouldn't come.

He wrapped himself in a cold, soggy sheet and fell asleep.

Spoons

for Archie Ammons

The landlord was always confused by spoons. When he helped his beautiful, big-breasted wife set the table, he'd stare at each spoon as if he'd never seen one before.

"Why do you always stare at the spoons?" his wife would ask.

"Oh, I don't know," he'd answer.

But the landlord did know.

Spoons reminded him of when he was a boy. How his father would pick up a spoon just before his mother came to the table and hold the back of the spoon up to the second knuckles of his middle and index fingers and ask, "Did you ever see your mother in the bathtub?"

The landlord had, in fact, seen his mother in the bathtub. But the reflection in the spoon looked nothing like her. He was not sure if the spoon showed her legs or her breasts or her buttocks.

To compound this confusion, his mother would come to the table, breathe deeply into the same spoon and stick it to her nose. "How do I look?" she'd ask, trembling with laughter.

He could always see, as his mother laughed, his father's face reflected in the spoon. His mother had a big nose and his father's reflection in the spoon looked more like his mother in the bathtub than did his father's knuckles held against the spoon that was hanging from his mother's nose.

When the landlord helped his beautiful, big-breasted wife set the table, he was confused by the spoons. No one had ever told him which side of the plate the spoon went on, and when he looked at a spoon, he forgot everything.

"I cannot understand," his wife would say, "why it is that you can't remember what goes where."

The Flannel Nightgown

He had been most kind. So the landlord did not understand why the boy had not told him what happened. Had he not allowed the boy to use his car? Hadn't he given him a condom so that he might protect himself from disease and other dangers? Had he not been almost a father to this boy? The answer to all these questions was yes, he had.

So why had the boy not described to him what had happened? And in minute detail? After all, it was his house. It was his car, his condom, his advice. Were boys these days no longer appreciative of what was given them? How rude to ignore the feelings of a kindly benefactor!

All that rainy Saturday the landlord worried. His beautiful, big-breasted wife could not occupy herself with washing the curtains, so she was at him constantly: "How come the pipes hammer every time I turn off the tap? What's that groaning noise when I flush the toilet?" He wanted to tell her that there was no explaining why the pipes hammered and groaned, but he knew she would not listen. No one listened anymore.

Late Saturday night the landlord heard the boy come in. There was much noise. The front door slammed and there were many heavy footfalls. He listened, but the boy said nothing. "Don't you know how to enter a house properly?" the landlord screamed down the steps, hoping the boy might want to talk. But there was no reply, not a sound.

He rolled over in his bed. His beautiful, big-breasted wife was snoring, her flannel nightgown rising with each shocked intaking of breath. He had not meant to be unkind, not really. But hell, there was such a thing as being polite, wasn't there? Why had the boy not shown a little gratitude?

The house was so silent. He wondered what the boy was doing. He wondered why it was the boy had been so inconsiderate. The landlord rolled onto his side and slipped his hand up under his wife's flannel nightgown to fondle her perfect breasts.

A Mother's Good Advice

Before the beautiful, big-breasted nurse became the landlord's wife--before she became a nurse, before she was big-breasted--she was, of course, a child. But even when she was a child, the landlord's wife was very beautiful.

She remembered always the day three of her mother's friends came to the house to play canasta. Her mother had dressed her in a pink dress with many crinolines. When her mother ushered her into the room where the women sat waiting, one of them said, "Such a beautiful child. Just look at that face."

"She will always be beautiful," said another, grasping her chin between thumb and forefinger.

"Oh no," said the third, "not if men have their way with her. If she is to remain beautiful, she must avoid the company of men!"

Then all the women laughed and began to deal the cards. "What must I do to remain beautiful?" she asked her mother the next day. Her mother was hanging out sheer lace curtains to dry in the spring sunshine.

Her mother thought for a moment and said, "Each morning you must drink camomile tea and when a man tries to put his hands on you, you must say this prayer: Jesus, I am yours alone; keep me sweet, Jesus."

When the landlord's wife grew up, she was pursued by young men who seemed always to want to put their hands on her breasts. But she followed her mother's advice. Each morning she drank a cup of camomile tea and when a young man tried to put his hands on her, she looked him directly in the eye and said: "Jesus, I am yours alone; keep me sweet, Jesus."

Other beautiful girls got pregnant and married men who treated them cruelly. These girls became women. They lost all their sweetness. But the landlord's wife remained as sweet as a child. Her mother's advice had, indeed, been good advice.

The Nightmare

That night the boy had a nightmare. In this nightmare he was back at school sitting next to the girl with the bad reputation. Her saddle oxfords had almost rotted away, so the boy knew that it was late spring. He was reading a book from his childhood, *The Tale of Peter Rabbit*, and he was staring at the illustration of Peter crawling under Mr. McGregor's garden gate. Mr. McGregor was chasing Peter. He had a rake in his hand. The boy was wondering why people hated each other and why there were always wars. Suddenly the air raid siren sounded.

The next thing the boy knew he was on the floor making passionate love to the girl with the bad reputation. With the toe of her right saddle oxford she was easing off the heel of the left. The boy heard one shoe clunk to the floor and then another. The boy was between the girl's legs; her dress was up and her scanties were down. "Hurry," she said, "before The Bomb comes." The boy looked at the girl. He was not making love to the girl with the bad reputation, he was making love to the landlord's beautiful, big-breasted wife! Just then the boy felt a hand on his shoulder. It was Mr. McGregor. But Mr. McGregor was the landlord! "What in God's name do you think you're doing? This is only a drill!" And the landlord brought the rake down on the boy's head.

The boy awakened and sat up in bed. Through his window he could see the landlord's wife was hanging out lace curtains to dry in the sun. The boy was frightened. He jumped out of bed and bolted into the hall where he ran smack into the landlord. "I had a terrible nightmare," the boy blurted. And he tried to tell the landlord about Peter Rabbit, the girl with the bad reputation (he did not mention the landlord's wife), the air raid siren, and the sound a rotten saddle oxford makes when it clunks to the floor. But the landlord had not read *The Tale of Peter Rabbit*, and he did not care to. He, in fact, disliked children's stories. Moreover, he never listened to other people's dreams and nightmares. He had enough of his own. He simply said, "Listen up: Dreams are not real. Go to the kitchen and get yourself some bread and milk and blackberries. You'll find some camomile tea warming on the eye."

George the Onion

When the landlord's wife was a young girl, there was a filthy old man who walked about the neighborhood with only his shorts and shoes on. No one liked this old man. He made obscene remarks, belched and broke wind when he encountered couples strolling, hand-in-hand, down the sidewalk. He leered at everyone.

One day the old man leered at the young girl who would later become the landlord's wife. She was playing in her mother's front yard. Without a word the old man lifted the hem of his pant leg and smiled. A testicle fell out. It was a filthy old testicle, all wrinkled and lanky. Then the old man cocked his leg and broke wind.

She ran into the house and told her mother what she'd seen. Her mother promptly called the police.

"What was the thing that fell out of the old man's pants?" she asked after her mother had hung up the phone.

Her mother thought for a moment. "That was George the Onion," she said. "All men have two onions: George the Onion and Albert the Onion. The one you saw sounds just like George."

"What do George and Albert do?" she asked.

Her mother kneeled down and took her by the shoulders. "They cause trouble," she said. "Especially the old ones. Young men have beautiful fresh onions. They are very pretty and smell quite sweet. But old men have nasty onions and they are the worst smelling things in the whole creation. You must always stay away from George and Albert when they get old. They will make you crazy."

She and her mother went into the front yard and found that the filthy old man was being forced into the back seat of a police car. "Get in there, you son of a bitch," an officer said, pushing the old man with his night stick.

As the police car pulled away from the curb, she waved. "Goodbye George, goodbye Albert."

The filthy old man stuck his head out of the car window and belched.

"See what I mean?" her mother said. "Old onions make people crazy."

III

Sheer Lace Curtains

Sheer Lace Curtains

The landlord's wife could remember when she was a small child. She remembered awakening in a crib and pulling herself up. It was a spring day. She knew this because in memory she was warm and the window at the end of the hall was wide open. It was very sunny and the sheer lace curtains were just stirring.

She remembered those lace curtains always. Her mother would wash them in the early spring. Sometimes, if the weather was perfect--sunny and just a bit breezy--her mother would hang the lace curtains out to dry. But if it was rainy or there was no breeze, her mother had a wooden frame from which protruded many small nails. Her mother would stretch the sheer lace curtains onto the frame to dry.

The curtains were always stiff with starch. Her mother cooked the starch on the stove and more than likely the starch would boil over and sizzle onto the eye. The clean curtains were very stiff. Until her mother hung them back in the windows. Then the curtains softened and lifted lightly in the breeze.

The landlord's wife could predict the weather by her lace curtains. When the curtains hung limp and gray, the day would be limp and gray. When the curtains lifted lightly in the breeze and the sky rose deep blue beyond the window, it would be spring-like. And when the curtains furled and fluttered, snapping like flags in a sudden wind, she knew there was a bad storm coming.

It took a great deal of work to keep the curtains stiff with starch and neatly pressed, but the landlord's wife did not mind. She kept them this way for the quiet moments they gave her. Once in a great while, when she walked into a room or climbed to the top of the stairs or rounded a corner, she'd happen upon herself. She was a child pulling herself up in her crib on a warm spring day. The sheer lace curtains were just stirring.

Rain or Shine

The boy had learned how things are when he was a child living with his parents in a small town.

Next door to the house where the boy lived there was a very large house owned by rich people. The man who lived in the house was the town mayor. He lived there with his wife and daughter, a girl some years older than the boy.

One day the father died. He had a heart attack and fell face down in the patch of daffodils. Not many weeks later his wife killed herself. Everyone in town was very sorry, but no one seemed concerned about the daughter. She was old enough to take care of herself, they said. Soon she sold the house and took an apartment nearby.

Every day, rain or shine, the daughter walked down the street and stood for hours staring at the house in which she had once lived with her parents. Spring, summer, fall, winter--she was always there.

This went on for many years, until the people of the town began to refer to the daughter as "Rain or Shine." Housewives could set their clocks by her; the postman knew when he had fallen behind schedule; townspeople gave directions using her as a reference point: "Take the first right after you pass Rain or Shine," they would say. She was that dependable.

One day a new family moved into the house, and they did not know the story of Rain or Shine. Moreover, they did not like being stared at. So they called the police. By this time most of the people in the small town had forgotten the daughter's story--or perhaps they simply no longer cared. The police put Rain or Shine in the back seat of a police car, and the boy never saw her again.

He asked his father why Rain or Shine had been taken away. "She never hurt anybody," the boy observed.

His father seemed irritated. "She was crazy," he said. "We can't have crazy people standing out in the street staring."

"Why not?" the boy asked.

His father thought for a moment and said, "Well, just because that's the way things are."

In time, the boy came to realize that his father was indeed a very wise man.

The Romantic Mountain Poet

The boy was not sure he always understood the poems written by the romantic mountain poet. But he had to admit that there was something about them, something that spoke directly to him. The poems were the very essence of spring, the sudden awakening, the honeysuckle in the shower and the dogwood blossoms pressing their sad faces against the fly-specked screen.

The boy opened the book and read slowly:

Ceres Rekindles

this weathered pelt of winter
tangled in the loamy root
this smoky tender blur
of budding leaf
this ancient rumor of spring
calls from the woods and rivers
the towns and cities
awaken to the crystal
clatter of laughter
drifting

the darting sparrow
the hands of sleeping lovers
leafage waxy and wild
red oak, poplar,
sycamore, silver maple, dogwood
the honeysuckle sings softly
sweet whispering spring!
sweet whispering death!

Whenever the boy read a poem by the romantic mountain poet, he saw everything more clearly.

He closed the book and stared out the window. The landlord was sitting under a tree drinking a bottle of beer. The lace curtains lifted lightly in the breeze. The sky rose deep blue, forever. All was right with the world.

There was a knock at his door.

Smiling

for Glen Rounds

When the boy was twelve years old, he began to wonder about breasts. The paperback books at the corner drug store had pictures of women on their bright glossy covers. These women all wore lacy low-cut dresses, and they all had very large breasts. It was these pictures that set the boy to wondering.

He began to notice the women who passed him on the street. What did their breasts look like? Were they bigger than they appeared? Were they smaller? Did they stick straight out? Were they soft? Were they hard? What did the nipples look like? It was difficult for a boy of twelve to know the answers to these questions. Breasts were the secret women carried with them everywhere. No wonder women smiled so often! They knew what all the men who looked at them wanted to know. Soon, however, the boy gave up trying to figure it out. It seemed there was no chance that he would ever see a real live breast. He began to believe that he might never know the answers to his questions. So he forgot all about breasts. Sort of.

Until the day his Aunt Amelia came to the house with her new baby. He asked to look at the child, and his aunt bent over so the boy could see clearly the child's face. The child was sucking at its mother's breast. The breast was very large and very white. The areola was dark against the child's pink lips. The child seemed to be smiling.

At first, the boy did not realize what he was looking at. Then a wave of shock and embarrassment washed over him. He had not intended to look at his aunt's breast. He had not meant to intrude at such an intimate moment. He tried to speak, tried to say something about how pretty the baby was. But only gibberish came out of his face: "Ah wo ugh woo aha. . . ." He ran to his room and locked the door.

After a few days, however, the boy got over his embarrassment. He grew curious again. He could not get the memory of his aunt's breast out of his head. It was so large and so white. And the child sucking it seemed so happy, so completely content. He began to feel that his curiosity was natural. And if his aunt did not mind, why should he?

On summer nights when the boy was twelve, he usually stayed out till after dusk. But let his Aunt Amelia show up with her new baby, and the boy was right there, the perfect gentleman, a smile on his face.

Wash Day

There was a knock at the boy's door. "It's wash day," he heard the landlord's wife say.

"Come in," he answered. The boy was sitting on the edge of his unmade bed, his chin resting in his hands.

"I must wash your curtains; it's that time of year," she said, cheerfully.

The boy did not answer.

"Is something the matter?" she asked.

"Yes," the boy said. And he tried to explain to the landlord's beautiful, big-breasted wife what it was he had been feeling. He told her what he felt about living in the house sided with cedar shakes and roofed with red tin. He explained to her about the romantic mountain poet. He described his evening at the drive-in with the girl and how he'd felt the next morning. He described for her the nightmare he'd had about sex and war (he did not mention, however, that she had been in the nightmare). "Nothing makes any sense," he said, beginning to cry. "I don't understand anything."

The landlord's wife smiled and sat down next to the boy on the unmade bed. She put her arm around him and drew his face close to her breast. Her blouse was slightly asunder. "There, there," she said, "you'll understand everything soon enough."

The boy looked up at the landlord's wife. She was smiling.

"You see," she said, pulling the boy down onto the bed, "you are troubled because you have taken all the sweetness from a young girl. . . ." She was fumbling with the buttons on her blouse.

"You must never put your hands on a sweet young girl."

The boy could not help himself. The lace curtains lifted lightly, unfurling gently above them.

Beer

What the landlord liked best about beer was that each bottle was better than the last. "Gosh," he would say after he'd finished a beer, "I believe that's the best one I've ever had!"

In the spring when the dogwood blossomed and his beautiful, big-breasted wife hung her curtains out to dry, the landlord liked to sit under a tree and drink lots of beer. The more beer he drank, the more he felt like a young boy. When he looked at his wife, he could feel the old juices beginning to flow. The air would be mild as milk, and the house, sided with cedar shakes and roofed with red tin, would stand neat and sturdy against the high blue sky.

This spring afternoon his wife was not hanging out her curtains, and the landlord wondered where she was. It was unlike her to not hang out her lace curtains on such a day. But after a couple of bottles of beer he forgot about his wife and his mind began to drift toward pipes and hot metal. He began to imagine the pipes running through the walls; he began to feel the cool heft of cast-iron 1/4 inch double bend; he could hear the sweet surge of gurgling water, the soft sighing of an open tap.

He looked at the dark windows of the boy's room. The bathroom window was smothered in honeysuckle; lace curtains lifted lightly in the window of the room where the boy slept. Small gray sparrows were singing in the dogwoods. The sky rose deep blue. All was right with the world.

When the landlord drank beer, he saw everything more clearly.

High Fidelity

When the landlord was fifteen, he was given a radio for his birthday. The radio was sealed in a cardboard box and when he opened the box there was a strange smell. He had never smelled anything like it. He plundered among the shredded newsprint and lifted the radio out. The radio had a plastic case the color of aged walnut. There were two dials: one was marked "volume" and the other "tuning." And there was an instruction booklet. The first page of the booklet said: "Congratulations! You will soon be enjoying High Fidelity."

He played the radio every night. Stations from distant parts of the world came in strong and true. There were strange voices speaking in languages he did not understand. There were opuses and comedies and many speeches by presidents and dictators. And he loved all that music about car wrecks and teenagers in love. On the summer nights when the room was warm, he wrapped ice in a towel and put it on top of the radio so that the cabinet would not melt. The radio was always there, a voice whispering in the darkness. A warm glow polka-dotted his bedroom wall.

One night the radio stopped playing. Only crackling noises came out. He unscrewed the brown fiberboard back and looked inside. One of the tubes, the big one in the very center of the radio, was dark. He wiggled the tube free and shook it. Something inside sounded like salt. He removed the other tubes and a small metal box wrapped in varnished wire. He grew curious and soon he had all the parts spread out on the floor. There was not much to it--five little tubes and a big one, a speaker, and the metal box wrapped in varnished wire. How could so much pleasure come from this odd assortment of glass, metal and plastic?

He read the instruction booklet carefully, but it did not tell how to put the radio back together. It explained how to plug it in and how to adjust the volume and how to tune in the stations. But that was all. On the first page it said: "Congratulations! You will soon be enjoying High Fidelity."

The Way Things Are

After the landlord's wife had gone, the boy sat up in bed and put his face in his hands. How could he have done such a thing? Had not the landlord been most kind? Had he not allowed him to live in his house? Had he not been almost a father to him? My God, the landlord had even allowed him to use his car. And he had given him a condom so that he might protect himself from disease!

Disease! The boy recalled the landlord's very words: "You'll need this to protect your plumbing." He had not worn a condom. There had been no time: things had literally gotten out of hand. So the boy went into the bathroom and turned on the shower. He opened the window and peaked through the honeysuckle. He brushed aside the blossoms and shooed the bees away. Thank God, the landlord was still sitting beneath a tree drinking a beer. All was quiet. Except for one small gray sparrow singing in a dogwood.

The boy washed his balls thoroughly, asking himself: What in God's name did I think I was doing? When he'd finished, he dressed and stuffed his shoes and clothes hurriedly into a pillowcase.

The boy knew that he must leave the landlord's house forever. But when he opened the door, there stood the landlord. "Would you like a cold beer?" the landlord asked.

"No thank you," the boy answered. "I'm moving out."

"I don't understand," the landlord said. "Why are you leaving?"

"Well," the boy said, "just because that's the way things are." And he handed the landlord the book of poems by the romantic mountain poet for whom it was always spring. "Here," he said, "you may have this book. It is entirely too cloying for me."

The boy clambered down the hall, creating much commotion and knocking over the umbrella stand. The landlord heard the door slam.

The Dead Sparrow

When the boy was nine years old he killed a sparrow. It was a small gray sparrow of the sort which constantly flitted about on the lawn in front of the boy's house. In one way, the killing of the sparrow had been an accident; in another way, it had been deliberate. Here is what happened.

The boy had purchased a two-bit slingshot from a toy store. The slingshot was made of wood and black strips of inner tube. For three or four days the boy was happy shooting rocks at road signs and mailboxes. He carried a pocket full of rocks and when he saw an interesting target, he let fly. He shot at clouds and trees and hubcaps and weather vanes. But alas, he was a terrible shot. The rocks always seemed to curve down and to the right, missing by inches what it was the boy was shooting at.

One morning the boy walked out on the front porch and saw a sparrow flitting about on the lawn. He pulled the slingshot from his back pocket and felt for a rock. There was just one. He let go at the very moment the sparrow took to flight. And to the boy's amazement, the rock curved up and to the left, striking the sparrow in the neck. The sparrow tumbled end over end and fell to the ground, a bundle of ruffled gray feathers.

The boy could not believe what he had seen. But when he pushed the small feathered body with the toe of his tennis shoe, it was obvious the sparrow was dead. The boy got a trowel and buried the sparrow, hoping no one would discover what he had done. Then he broke the slingshot into pieces and threw it into a ditch.

For days the boy was troubled by the death of the sparrow. Soon, however, he came to understand that it was not his fault. Had not the rock curved up and to the left? And why was there just one rock in his pocket that morning? And why had the rock caught the sparrow just as it had taken to flight? It was obvious to the boy that the sparrow's death had nothing to do with him.

Still, when he walked by the spot where he had buried the sparrow, the boy closed his eyes tight. But no matter how hard he tried not to see, the sparrow was always there--a small bundle of ruffled gray feathers tumbling end over end.

Of Course and as Always

The landlord found his wife fast asleep. She was wearing her flannel nightgown and muttering to herself over and over: "Keep me sweet, Jesus. Keep me sweet...."

He wandered into the bathroom and opened the tap. The pipes groaned and rattled. He splashed cool water on his face, opened the medicine cabinet and removed the bottle of bay rum. He shook some into his hand, rubbed his hands together briskly, and he ran his fingers through his hair. He took a deep breath.

He did not understand why the boy had left. So many young men had come and gone, all of them departing in such haste. He had been most kind to all his young boarders--he'd been, in fact, almost a father to each and every one. Young people these days were just not appreciative.

He watched his wife's sheer lace curtains, freshly ironed and stiff with starch, lift lightly in the breeze. Honeysuckle blossoms, thick and sweet as cream, rattled against the gauzy, fly-specked screen. Green tendrils drifted imperceptively up the wavy blue-green glass, tangling between the sashes, entwining. The sky rose deep blue beyond the window.

No, he did not understand--but, then, not understanding was something the landlord understood. It was a lesson he'd learned long ago. It had stood him in good stead all his life.

Stephen E. Smith was born in Easton, Maryland, in 1946. After graduating from Elon College, he attended the University of North Carolina at Greensboro, where he received his MFA in 1971. He is the author of *The Bushnell Hamp Poems* and a book of stories, *The Great Saturday Night Swindle*. In 1981, he was awarded the *Poetry Northwest* Young Poet's Prize. He lives in Southern Pines, North Carolina and teaches at Sandhills Community College.

Glen Rounds was born in the Badlands of South Dakota and spent his boyhood on a horse ranch in Montana. He has worked all around the country as a sign painter, cowpuncher, mule skinner, logger, carnival barker, and lightning artist. He has illustrated well over a hundred books, many of which he has also written, and he has been awarded the 1980 Kerlan Award from the University of Minnesota and the 1981 North Carolina Award for Literature. He lives in Southern Pines, North Carolina.